D1215453

Grace Art:
Poems and Paintings

by:

Grace Cavalieri

Poets' Choice

Poets' Choice Publishing

Copyright © 2021 Poets' Choice Publishing
All rights reserved.

Graphic Design: Sanket Patel

Paintings and Poems: Grace Cavalieri

Photo Credit: Dan Murano

Printed in the United States of America
Library of Congress Cataloging-in-Publication Data Pending

ISBN # 978-1-7335400-9-4

Cover Painting:
"Uschi Nottnagel"
Mixed Media
By Grace Cavalieri

Poets' Choice

Poets' Choice Publishing
337 Kitemaug Road
Uncasville, CT 06382
Poets-Choice.com
marathonfilm@gmail.com

Grateful acknowledgment to:

Online magazine DCTrending.com for the Grace Cavalieri interview:

"The Covid Poetry & Art Project"

Dan Murano for technical assistance with visuals.
The owners of Cavalieri paintings for reproduction permission.

CONTENTS

Pandemic Paintings, An Introduction
by Richard Harteis

I got an email from Grace Cavalieri recently, who said she was surviving the pandemic by color. There's a poetic explanation for you! (Grace is the Poet Laureate of Maryland, of course, so it's the kind of response one might expect.) There are many individual ways to survive lockdown, but Grace seems to have drawn from her inner resources to tap yet another vein in her artistic gold mine.

At the Bread Loaf Writers' Conference one summer, a revolution broke out between conservatives like John Ciardi, and progressives like William Meredith who believed the function of criticism was to illuminate a work of art, to translate the artistic talent for readers not familiar with the innovation a new artist creates. The purpose of criticism was not to say what is good or bad. You did not need to embarrass a student to encourage them. Love and support were called for from a good teacher.

I guess I rely on the old chestnut, "I know what I like when I see it." And boy, do I like these wonderful paintings, so full of life and color. Perhaps only a poet could include such wit and obsessional attention in the objects she finds to include in the paintings. Like Maya Angelou, she knows why the caged bird sings. In one poem she describes silence as the mother of all muses. And it's in this silence that she has created these beautiful poems and paintings. "Art makes us less lonely," runs the cliché, and sharing her loneliness makes the reader less lonely.

One of my favorite commercials on TV these days (I admit I watch too much TV, haven't found a better use of my time the way Grace has done in the meditative silence she lives in while creating these works) a father and his daughter are seen spritzing ketchup and mustard all over a hot dog and themselves. Mom walks in and rolls her eyes asking for an explanation. The small daughter looks at the Jackson-Pollock-like hot dog and says it's "art lessons, Abstract Expressionism."

I hesitate to "pigeonhole" these works, (think Klee, think Miro,) but I am convinced they require a larger audience than the family and friends who are lucky enough to own one of these pieces. And these painting are not ment to be illustrations of a paticular poem, rather they are like "going on a date," as the poet says. The paintings are not just a deserving use of her time, but what she has accomplished in facing the blank canvas as she has faced the blank page.

What follows is an interview by Norah Vawter from DCTrending online magazine (DCTrending.com) which gives you Gracie in her own words. How lucky we are to have this talented angel singing for us in the wilderness.

Online Magazine DCTrending.com
Interview by Norah Vawter

Grace Cavalieri:
The COVID Poetry & Art Project

Grace Cavalieri is Maryland's tenth poet laureate. During quarantine, she's also started painting and has shared with us both a painting and poem. And if you want to read more of Grace's pandemic poetry: she's one of the amazing poets featured in 2021 anthology Singing in the Dark: A Global Anthology of Poetry under Lockdown.

Chatting with Grace

Can you tell us a little about this poem or piece of art and how you came to create it? How has the current crisis (or crises) influenced your art?

I am sharing a painting, one of the 50 I have produced during this last year of seclusion. It was certainly a time where there was nothing left to lose but loneliness, so I added that relaxing regimen to augment my daily writing practice. And why did I dare? Because the great poet A. R. Ammons once said, "If you are nothing, you can say and do anything." So, I knew I had the credentials! Autobiography was accepted by a gallery in Chicago but then a bubble was detected under the paint. I smile because there are many bubbles. I have three failed paintings under this one and finally settled for half collage before discarding it. The paper inclusions all speak to me about my life: books, cats, fun, activism, poetry. It secretly contains tiny slices of favorite poets also. Poetry comes from a quiet place and I think "View" reflects that. Clearly, it starts from a "point of view," with the speaker looking out the window and describing what is seen or intuited. But the voice, which goes out into silence, here comes back into poetry.

What role do you think the arts play in times of turmoil and uncertainty?

Turmoil makes art! And when faced with the ultimate wall (living alone for a year), there was nothing for me to do but paint a window on that wall. And then keep going every day as a discipline (discipline in meaning "disciple to").

What are you viewing/reading/watching/listening to these days?

In the meantime, books are our friends and do not have germs. So I'll just name those read during the past few weeks. Plays: The Liar by Pierre Corneille, plus a modern adaptation, The Liar by David Ives. Collections of poems: by Jack Gilbert, Ruben Dario and Su Tung-P'o. Also history: The Grandmother Of Jesus, and the new Washington Writers' Publishing House Anthology, "This Is What America Looks Like." Finally, art is the result of a great mysterious gift from the cosmos raining down light and animating everything. All we have to do is make something to connect to the divine. It's a collaboration and doesn't depend on winning any prizes to do what we do. Art brings us together. The poetry workshops I have on zoom have brought daily energy into my room and filled me with that light. It makes family, community, tribe--something to share--and, as has been said, art makes us less lonely.

Do you have a favorite local writer or artist (DC area)?

I love the poets in the DC/Maryland/Virginia area! It's the poetry capital of the world.

About The Artist

Grace Cavalieri is Maryland's tenth Poet Laureate. Grace is the author of 26 books and chapbooks of poetry and 20 short-form and full-length plays. A book of her paintings is forthcoming from Poet's Choice Press. Her latest book of poems is What The Psychic Said, (Goss publications 2019,) previous books are Showboat, about 25 years as a Navy wife (Goss;) and Other Voices, Other Lives (ASP, 2018.). Her latest play "Quilting The Sun" was produced at the Theater for the New City, NYC in 2019. She founded and produces "the Poet and the Poem" for public radio, now from the Library of Congress, celebrating 44 years on-air. Among other honors Grace holds The Associated Writing Program's George Garrett Award, plus the Pen-Fiction, the Allen Ginsberg, Bordighera Poetry, and Paterson Poetry awards; the "Annie" Award; The inaugural Folger Shakespeare Library Columbia Award; The National Working Women Commission Award, and The CPB Silver Medal.

DCTrending.com

Grace Art:

Poems and Paintings

VIEW

My sacred space, a bird flying to the feeder
the shade of a tree, berries in the forest
heat from the sun on the pane
flames of experience
lashing on glass
the clear path of vision
the straight edge of sky
a parting of water
picking us up placing us exactly there
history has been shattered into pieces that will not fit together
how large is loss
how much does it take to fill
how do we gather it in our arms
when the city was destroyed with illness there was a place I could not reach
right now a small animal is breaking free in the woods
the milk of the moon is shining on these words that come from me
and do not return empty.

Berries
16" x 20"
Acrylic on canvas

STUNNED

I don't know about dropping a full bottle of wine on the pavement in Pisa
Or both leaving our hats in the locker room in Maryland on the same day
Or talking about our neighbor in West Virginia who killed his cat
As we stand hand in hand looking
At the milk of the moon shining on the whole world
I alive— you dead—saying if this could happen, anything could.

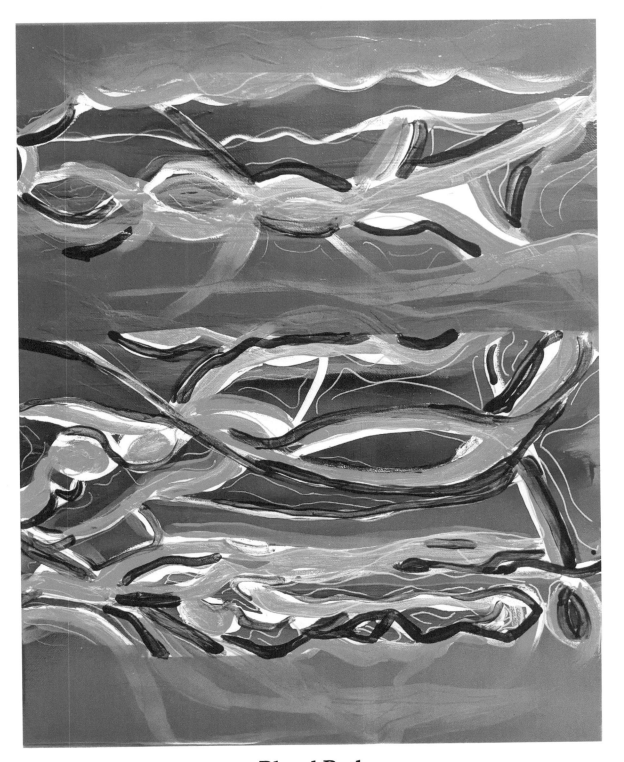

Blood Path
16" x 20"
Acrylic on canvas

12: 45 ON A FRIDAY

I looked in my address book
to see who I was.

The wild cat of the past
is all I saw—

I felt the pages again.
A to Z were poised to my finger.

Midsummer late winter early spring

Even the stars have lost their
memories.

The red from the Hummingbird
will show life a little ease—

I almost went fishing on a boat to Key West
but I never called him back.

Bryan
16" x 20"
Acrylic on Canvas

THE LIBERATION OF MUSIC

When someone brought
Anthony Braxton flowers
He didn't frown
And he didn't ask if
They were
Picked off a tree.

Like this tear
On my eye
Becoming a circle
Which I flick off my cheek
Just like that
With my nail

Removing the last flaw
Which holds my life together.

Burst
16" x 20"
Acrylic on Canvas

THE LAST PAINTING

We passed his new painting around the room—
A ship embroidered with the glory and movement of time—
"It needs a title," I say, "some signal for the reader."
He whispers, "the picture says I'm going away."
To cover sudden silence, I say, "I'll help you pack."

In youth we thought art was a metaphor.
We go upstairs, saying goodbye to our friends.
They think we're going to make love one more time.
But we are too old and we just lie there side by side.
We just lie that way until the canvas is empty.

Color of Berries
16" x 20"
Acrylic on Canvas

A WELL KNOWN THING

(for Ken)

I was confined to my youth
giving the empty sky my attention
and you murmured something
impeccable, I'll never forget—

Careless, before you,
trapped and rooted.
Thank you for this— transcended—
Rarified— once Love's beggar
now its belief.

Dan's Painting
11" x 14"
Acrylic on Canvas

BEYOND ITS POSSIBILITIES

Loneliness is not exactly solitude.
Solitude is not exactly loneliness, as each
presses forward into the other,
chased by a conference of philosophical opinions
under the weight of perhaps too much thought.
Let us say, rather, what feelings are let flying
all at once in the flinty grey of dawn—
—well that's the way I'd rather go in any
garden of discussion— what rises high in the heart
and falls low, unexpectedly, without management
—and what coexists with surprise.

Diagnosis
16" x 20"
Acrylic on Canvas

SINGING FOUNTAIN

Sometimes when a yellow umbrella is not enough
and the emerald in the grass is just broken glass
and I'm missing romance and have only
its memory flawlessly executed
the sun showers through anyway
and everyone who was ever dead is alive again
rinsing their hands with rain, saying
we're here now. There's work to do. And we do.

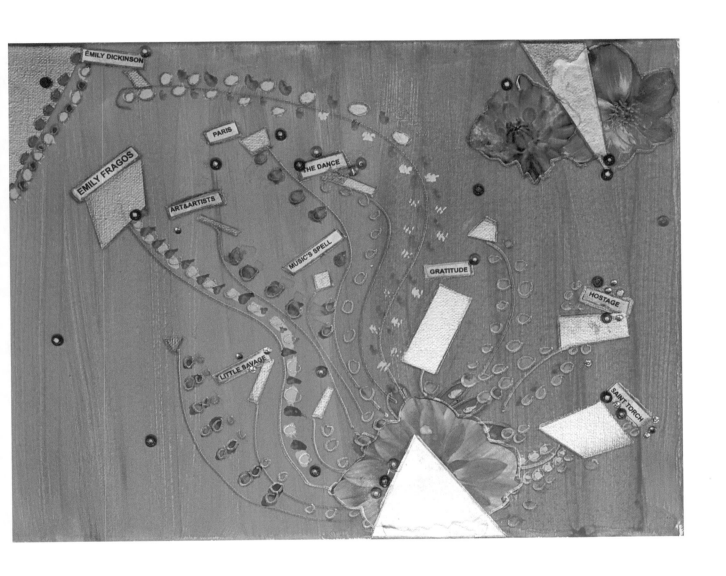

Emily Fragos
Mixed Media

VOYAGES

This poem never went to Africa
to sleep on the floor of the tent
or to treat children for scurvy.
This poem didn't even get as far as
Mexico where it could nestle
under the white hot sun in the warm
brown sand.
In fact, this poem's never been
anywhere at all and has led
a rather sheltered life,
but then again Daring comes
from within as a famous poet
once said,
and like the red flower blooming
on an otherwise green prickly stalk
flames up to the top,
radiant, and brilliant, as one who dares
to give away the precious pebbles of her life
and someone else who dares to take them.

Escape
16" x 20"
Acrylic on Canvas

BENEVOLENCE

How good and true the light is,
How it never lets us down,
Showing up again and again,
Every single day, from every single night,
How it is fair to everyone, rich and poor alike,
And how much,
How very much it makes me love the sky,
Because it will always be there.

Flow
16" x 20"
Acrylic on Canvas

GUARDIAN OF TIME

I don't know how I knew this –
This deepening love – subjectivity of experience –
The desolation of the prairie rabbit –
How the sky and the air can turn pink
For no reason.
We would not have seen the pink
Unless there were sun beaming down, its
Wishes closing in, guarding our treasures,
Answering the question:
How to love without fear
Just look at the ball of sun behind the tree
Now a deepening orange
Now a fanning behind the branches
Like images in God's dream—
Did you think there was an easier access to happiness?

Flowing
16" x 20"
Acrylic on Canvas

HAIKU

From the sky's
Shorelines
All the stars fall out

Forensics
11" x 14"
Acrylic on Canvas

LUNATICS

Rivers like veins taken by night
By what we remembered now dry
Leaving their shadows leaving our shadows
Behind a big achievement for the sun
Which will be remembered for our failures
Once the Anglicized air was sweet and pure
Now a scar on our cheeks of smoke
Touch it we are the lunatics who
Slept with moonlight on our faces
Legend says that makes you crazy
And indeed dry land dead water we
Must have been.

Grace
Acrylic on Canvas

THE ZEN STICK

Please do not let the man in the wheelchair stop
to look into a store window at shoes,

rather watch the girl carry
an arm full of sunflowers.

Don't you know regret eats the empty air,
while garbage makes sunflowers grow.

Everything makes everything else.

The candle makes wax.
The wax makes the smoke

from which
sparks start again.

Gloria Al Masri
Mixed Media

PULLED ALONG BY THE MOON

The asparagus is growing to the sky indifferent to earth
A letter to nowhere
The squirrel delivers a leaf to my husband in thanks for past meals
No one is here
Do you remember the time the wisteria grew inside the back door
It had to be cut
And now the Azalea is back with a chorus of fire with a hummingbird
Romancing the feeder
In the pastures of Heaven we are told there is no sorrow—that even in this
Sandstorm there's something to praise
I am told we should thank Winter for all this— I guess it is something like thanking
Death for his life.

Unknown
Acrylic on Canvas

JUST THIS

From the palest soil
After the cold of night
Within the shape of day
The edge of paradise
Flaming Winter's hill
Moving with the morning
Earthly beauty
Ready for eternity

If we walk a journey
Where will it lead
Or is the path the path
Where there is no harm
Merely the comfort
Of leaning in
Surrendering

Shelley Flynn
Mixed Media

MUDRA

Every day I wake to find that I know nothing
The next day I find that I know even less
Today I learned that when I wake to consciousness
The cat will come to me
He doesn't need to see my open eyes
Today I learned the right hand on the
Heart will calm its beating
I will not know this until I touch my heart
Tomorrow again I will know nothing
I will trust the cat, the heart

Rachel Price

Mixed Media

TELL ME A STORY IN ANY LANGUAGE

Tell me about that "God," again, the phantom that
I let out of heaven, unlocking him from people's thoughts,
how as a young woman I sat in a metal chair on the hill
by a green tree, watching the random glance of sun slice
across a lace of grass, a fountain of air,
watching for God to get out of there. This is
brushing up against the laws of nature, I thought,
but went to the verge of sorrow, returning from tomorrow
with its plane of memory, its fading words,
we have to sit somewhere, why not there?

Dylan Price
Mixed Media

THE LADY READS MY PALM

It's not luck you need to read the stars. It's the
shape of sorrow in your cup.
You once saw the wild ground
turn to shells beneath your feet.
You saw the gorgeous salt of the ocean
turning blue. You walked on melting sand and
now the lonely fervor quiets.
Make sense of this love where rock becomes air.
Who will sit with you.
Who will read your poems.
He said he is sorry.
Please take back your ring.
 It's worth more than paper, gold or cash.
There's a song inside your finger
saying more than a letter.
Take love.
Hold it to your ear and you will see
a vision.
The shepherd moves across the fields.
You'll hear a name calling you home.

Janice Booth
Mixed Media

ADVICE REGARDING A FIELD
OF REINDEER IN THE SNOW

If your husband is sleeping, you
can leave him a message and go in
the airplane with the mysterious pilot,
just for an hour, to land in strange
cities, farmlands, perhaps with
wet leaves and wooden
houses, with ruffled curtains.
You may walk to the edge
of what you thought was a forest,
and look through a thick wall of ice
with a gigantic hole and see
field after field of reindeer brushed
with snow, standing still,
how beautiful, like frozen statues,
cold and silent, each staring straight at you,
line after line of them,
a sight you'd never have seen
had you stayed home. You'll never forget it,
but remember to leave a note, before you go, or
your return will be bleak,
it will ruin everything: trip, field, reindeer, snow.

Colleen Flynn
Acrylic on Canvas

JAPANESE CATS

In Haiku there is one rule: no cats.
They are too cute, too easy to win our love.
That's the rule.
Yet today
my cat saw the blossoms blow
and begged
to go outside,
but first he turned to sniff his food
one last time.

This is not a haiku for
I have more I want to say:

I want to talk about my Beloved
who left before the dawn overlapped the sky—
how first he stopped to conjure one last sight.
We'd settled to a life
that no one could dissolve,
We entered it together in a bubble
floating toward a needle,
before a second stolen

turning back
before the blossoms.

Vickie Rudow
Acrylic on Canvas

HARBINGER

You'll never get it finished
Don't even try
You can never return a life payment of kindness and hurt
You'll never arouse
your first love again
You'll never learn the geography
Of the archipelago or name
Those yellow flowers shaped like angels by the side of the road
And you don't even care anymore
About who bought you the white straw hat
You'll never visit the snow in Russia
Or play chess
Or service a computer
Forget it
Not in this lifetime
Your skin will never be soft and pink as your first child's
Nothing is left
So just be good
Don't try to be good.
BE Good. How? Don't ask
Just do it
The rest is none of your business.

Avideh Shashaani

Acrylic on Canvas

COVID HAIKU

Points on a map
Growing smaller now
Window porch street

Shelley Flynn
Acrylic on Canvas

HAIKU

At the columbarium
The Bee buries itself
In the flower

Shelley Flynn
Acrylic on Canvas

HAIKU

Long dark winter
Covid
Zoom me baby

Rose Solari

Mixed Media

RAIN OF LIGHT

This is how it happened:
The moon was new. There was
joy peace patience kindness
generosity faithfulness.
Each bird, even while eating tiny seeds,
was watching for predators.
I don't think I was looking
for something myself but who
knows why I stayed there,
maybe waiting it out
to see if the hawk would come and scatter the flock.
Maybe I had nowhere else to go
or maybe I thought of saying this.
Whatever I was thinking I cannot
remember now but for that scene
of the finches and titmice
until finally of course I came in from the dark.

Maria Van Beuren
Acrylic on Canvas

PORTRAIT OF A LADY GOING TO HEAVEN

Close Your eyes
Reflect on the horizon the absolute blue
Take your footprints off the earth and hurl them upward
Concentrate
Against running or jumping
That won't help
Wobble like a moth against reality
Never mind crawling up a cliff
Or fluttering out a 30-story building
Float harmony on air instead
Breathe faith instead of swallowing
Hemlock or plucking nightshade
Remember ordinary love
When he put his hand over yours
You were afraid of an event
And he said
Don't Worry I'll Get You There.

Elaine Arata
Mixed Media

OF COURSE IN THE DISTANCE

If I hold out my hand and give you a key no matter how far I reach there is no one to lift the latch beyond the door there is no key no hand and all that remains is the air you wanted and could not hold the way I pretended there was a key and the door and someone to open it.

Barbara Quick
Mixed Media

LEARNING FROM BUDDHA

The cat likes to lick
a piece of butter
at the end of a knife
propped up by the window
so he can watch the birds
today I forgot the butter and the knife
he didn't care
he knows
some days
there are no birds.

Bela De May

Mixed Media

AWARDS DAY

She always wanted to make love to a clock so she'd know
when to stop. She always wanted to be standing in the
limelight in a white satin dress, no, make that a strapless dress.
Now she was older and, so no, make that one with sleeves.
She wanted to be a cat hiding in a tree to catch a bird.

Autobiography
Mixed Media

DEAR WORD PRISONER

From here you can see the water past craggy purple
rocks, stretches of green, rusted roof tops,
limned fields— yet this is not enough—
Spirits need language and what does it matter
unless we can describe the outdoor air at dark,
the late-night owl or fox,
walls leaning thick with loss,
stones large with dirt and leaves and moss—
Many souls lived and walked here on their way to heaven.
What led them on, glittering with love or luck?
Tell me what world we can speak of if not this,
the roaring of the ocean,
the emptiness of winter's gate—
I've visited these places but left
for all the words that could not touch them.
Anything! I say! Squeal, cry, yelp, sigh out loud,
say something, mouth, say Summer,
talk of hands that held here. Whose?
The convert feathers rest silent in the tree
for lack of sound from heart.
Dear tongue, breath:
Don't leave me here alone with all this disappearing.

Nicole Roberts

Mixed Media

MAKING TORTILLAS SHAPED
LIKE YOUR HEART

Carve some starved corn

out from the Harvest moon

and throw in some wild flowers—

Chain the bowl to the arch of wind

then sleep against the wall

until the perfect date to bake—

Turn and whirl in a wide wide skirt

and stir the spoon as you go –

Pour heavily into the beggar's bowl

then donate yourself to the sun.

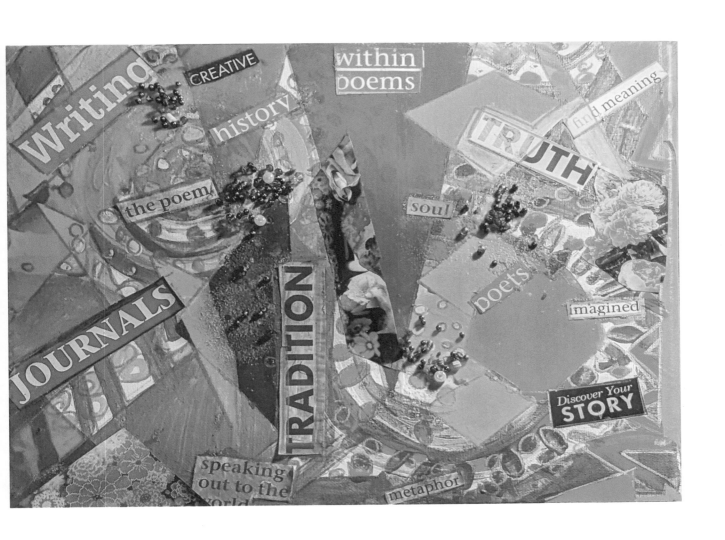

Miss Dinasta
Mixed Media

ELEGIES FOR THE NEW YEAR

I woke up with sun on my face and said
to Ken
Let's Go To Key West

Katherine Wood
Mixed Media

COLOSSUS

The House We Built

It started with carnations he gave me - age 16
And how they multiplied by the hundreds
Making a mosaic basement for our house
Of course we knew the fragility and decay
How easily they could be crushed
But the glass stair to the first floor was found where
We walked carefully- so much luggage from our childhood- until
Finally secure on Floor One -above the drifting past- we found the
Next floor- the children--the lightning of love-- the danger of sorrow
And then the place above this – music - swirling skirts - yellow cars
Riding pink through the sunsets of Key West toward
The roof where we stood in the mist - sun -hail - with
The house crumbling beautifully away.

Claire Cavalieri
Mixed Media

HAIKU

Scarlet Autumn
Purses lips
One last kiss

Uschi Nottnagel
Mixed Media

MIGRATIONS

Open wide the windows
     from the high tower
caught as I am in mid-air
     green still stands outside
inside the children's empty boots
     left beside the door
in my dream those
     voices coming up the hill
toward me
     children clamoring in
with bundles larger
     than the heart
let us have lunch
     where is the milk
can I tell you a story
     how I stood beneath
the stairs and lowered my eyes
     so as not to cry.

Migrations
Mixed Media

WHY THE DALAI LAMA LAUGHS

After awareness for the poor, the disinherited, the shamed
    then, there is compassion.

After compassion for others
    there is self–compassion.

After the Self can release its pain
    then suffering will change to calm.

Then comes happiness. After happiness, there is
    awareness. Then, there is compassion…

Unknown
Acrylic on Canvas

ENLIGHTENMENT

I am told to breathe into the world
inside myself.
Attachment equals a fixed point of view.
I should be mindful when I eat, for the sun and soil brought the food.
I must walk slowly with meditative steps to reach my destination.
I water the seeds of joy every day.
I can hold my suffering like a small child
and calm the world.
I can know compassion on either side of the gun.
I think of Yeats
"Things reveal themselves passing away,"
that emotions come and go,
they depend on the wind, the weather, the sound of the rain,
but as I sip my tea
no matter how near or far away
I know I'm writing with a borrowed pen,
my feelings are fireflies that will vanish in the sky.
Even so, under the slivered moon, I still want the hand of tenderness,
remembering the poet who wrote, "do what you can with this."

Cindy Cavalieri
Acrylic on Canvas

LANGUAGE

What's there to say about the rose,
and the dew inside the rose—
Who can see the simplicity

of hidden light, the unmarked flower –
light, dew, rose do not know
the names for their slight lives.

That's why we watch in silence
without a need for speech—
the sun doesn't know why it's called sun

No matter what is said
we learn by stillness—
all that's beautiful will grow.

Ladi Di
Mixed Media

SILENCE, THE WAY IT HOLDS THE TRUTH

Silence, wanderer, you, with your purposeful imagery –
Nothing inflames the past as much as you do!
How many places can you lead the mind at once –
Perception? (Oh, now you look down) – Invention?
(Now you nod) – So much you hold, to darkness,
then to bliss.
Look at this collection of poems –most expressive,
don't you think? Various patterns fused together? All
with Silence. So, how many
different directions do you own, replenished by words?
You surround language with sensuality as if you were alive.
You want to do us in,
your ceaseless spirit, avoiding my gaze,
taking us down the road with you.
Silence, the mother of all muses,
always the winner, in wait for us, with your cunning,
treating me to the final word.

Patch
16" x 20"
Acrylic on Canvas

A FIELD OF FINCHES WITHOUT SIGHT STILL SINGING

That song comes from sorrow there is no doubt.

Bullfinches in ancient times had eyes put out

so they would sing more sweet. Think of

those black beads dropped to earth coming

to seed flowers turning inward every single

one of them without its sight.

Stories say that moving in the wind they

made up song as if nothing had been lost and

this rings long into the night. Every sound

we hear turns to a bigger one and each is

true. We add our own until it is the first

din ever heard, the way poetry begins.

Maria Van Beuren
Mixed Media

A GREEN GHAZAL

Green grass rises and rises season after season
my husband's heart there season after season

green is the color of my true love's hair
I hear a ticking under the earth season after season

I closed the green hospital curtains and said "Rest"
then "NO! WAIT!" I think of this season after season

when young I lost my gold Bulova watch in the ocean
ticking in green foam season after season

legends are based on these small parts of the voice
how the range of oceans is big and fearless season after season

 bushes stay green after Azalea blossoms float away
this is graceful of Spring before leaving season after season

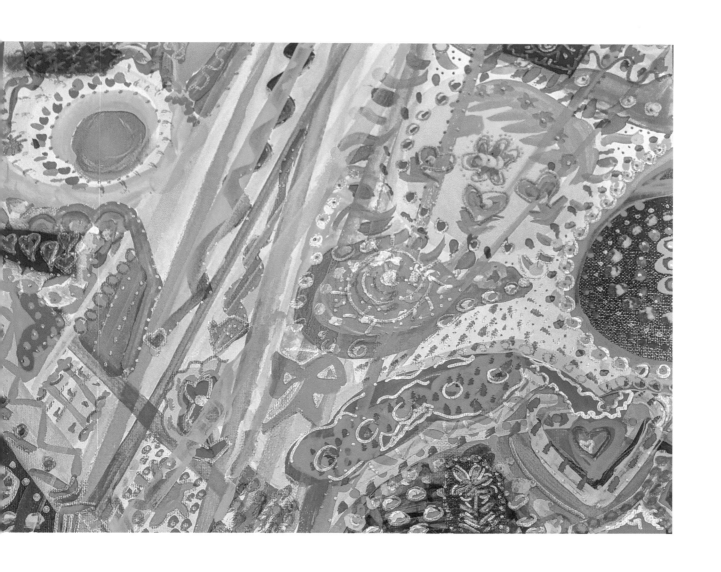

Candace Katz
Acrylic on Canvas

HAIKU

Buttercup doesn't know
It grows under a Sun
Not knowing it shines

Joe Phelan
Mixed Media

CAN I COUNT ON YOU

If I were lying in a boat in a wedding gown would you see me floating by

If I named a star after you would you lie in the grass looking up

If I lived in a white house would you come sit on my front porch

If I were caught in a bad dream would you please wake me up

If I had a plaid blouse would you help me button it

If I could jitterbug would you do the double dip

If I were a red cardinal would you hold out a sunflower seed

If I caught all the fireflies in the world would you give me a big jar

If the night nurse forgets to come would you bring me a glass of water

If I have only minutes to look at the silky moon will you come get me

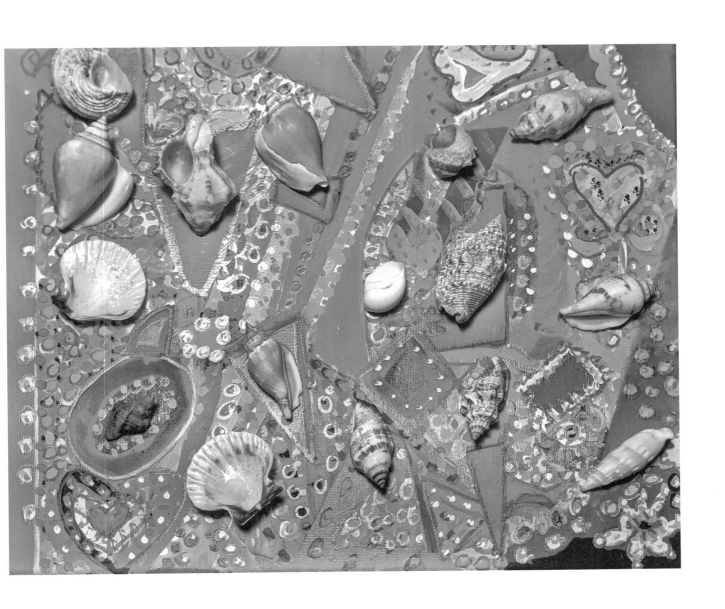

Ann Bracken
Mixed Media

BLUEBIRDS

In the small grey hut of self-doubt where the ceilings are too
low for you to stand,
by the road where your friend would only drive you half-way home,
next to the trench of holes filled with grief and wrong choices,
where it's better not to know how you should do things a different way,
tulips droop from their vases,
and death has never had so many faces.

That's the time to go out at dusk when even the deaf talk softly;
Don't look at the hummingbird hovering
afraid of the bubbles rising in their nectar—
Bluebirds know of danger, their air made of smoke–
large wings of prey
never far distant—
Try to find the bluebirds in their church of air,
star seeds of sound that crystallize then burst.

Serenity
Acrylic on Canvas

MAMA DIDN'T ALLOW NO BLUES OR JAZZ

The monkey trap is simply this
A coconut hollowed out
A sweet potato stuck inside

This is how a monkey can be caught
He puts his paw inside
And grabs his food

You say it's dumb
Determined as hunger
Caught inside a shell like that

You say betrayal comes from just
Such needs as a monkey has

We do not know the source of sanity
How monkeys feel about hunger

But I think it's better when holding on
From not letting go
I think it's better to let go.

Silver
11" x 14"
Acrylic on Canvas

TAKE MY IMAGINATION

Friend of my mind, take my thoughts where you cannot
yourself imagine and try to go inside coming toward yourself
not through epic narratives nor astronomical equations
but piece by piece small fragments
justice or injustice it doesn't matter
they are just words we don't have to understand
what we love don't worry about what is fair or right
please know I'm just doing my job expanding myself through you
this is my mission reminding you who you are
who you were meant to be one by one the vision
wanting our hearts to be free this is my poetic material
only this not lyric not verse something better
chasing you down scorching your secret life asking
what can you hear this moment? a poetic performance?
or a cure? whatever it is break open and see what's inside
say it out loud and dare to make it yours.

Stained Glass
16" x 20"
Acrylic on Canvas

A VISIT TO THE SUN

The bottom land is the richest land
lighted by the hidden moon.
I see deep sediment with its eternal silence.
All we feel is waiting to bloom there.
The sun lifts from its horizon.
For one long day, dreams rise from
the excavation site of the heart.
The first thing I notice is the light. Then
the tide comes in. The river is full,
and a lost world comes into sight.
Carved by desire, its rapture
presses fingers to my eyes,
leaving tiny indentations.
Did you think the real world was all there was?
Did you think Love came from nothing?
I disappear as if by magic.
Nothing in my life will ever be the same.

Transparency
16" x 20"
Acrylic on Canvas

ONCE UPON A HUMMINGBIRD

Soon we thought we
Knew everyone we needed to know
The glistening berries on a card
The new lawn, its quiet

After we walked on the
Confetti of crepe myrtle
There was nothing we could not trespass

Far from sleep came
A return from the distance
Tiny breezes, waiting trees
Petals released

Now before Autumn
A red cup for the smallest of birds
Before migration across eternity
Flying the ocean

For this hour I wondered
What Forever looked like
Now I know it's an epiphany
Above the door sipping sugar water

Whirring from silence
Saying what we had to forgive
Before leaving.

Wrightville Beach
16" x 20"
Acrylic on Canvas

CPSIA information can be obtained
at www.ICGtesting.com
Printed in the USA
BVHW020059060421
604264BV00004B/18